Card art

Create Treasured Greetings from Fabric & Paper

Susan S. Terry

C&T PUBLISHING

LOVE USA 55

Text © 2006 Susan S. Terry

Artwork © 2006 Susan S. Terry

Publisher: Amy Marson

Editorial Director: Gailen Runge

Acquisitions Editor: Jan Grigsby

Editor: Lee Jonsson

Copyeditor/Proofreader: Wordfirm, Inc.

Cover Designer: Christina Jarumay

Book Designers: Staci Harpole, Cubic Design and Kiera Lofgreen

Design Director: Staci Harpole, Cubic Design

Illustrator: John Heisch

Production Assistant: Kiera Lofgreen

Photography: Diane Pedersen and Luke Mulks, unless otherwise noted

Published by C&T Publishing, Inc., P.O. Box 1456, Lafayette, CA 94549

Front and Back covers: All cards are designed and made by Susan S. Terry

Library of Congress Cataloging-in-Publication Data

Terry, Susan S.
  Card art : create treasured greetings from fabric & paper / Susan S. Terry.
      p. cm.
  Includes index.
  ISBN-13: 978-1-57120-350-2 (paper trade)
  ISBN-10: 1-57120-350-8 (paper trade)
  1. Greeting cards. 2. Textile crafts. I. Title.

TT872.T47 2006
745.594'1--dc22   2005029856

Printed in China

10 9 8 7 6 5 4 3 2 1

contents

where are you art?

I started my cardmaking career by attempting to paint cards using Chinese watercolor painting techniques. (I don't have an art background. As a child I was lucky if I could locate two crayons in our house at any given time, and if I did, they were the same color.) A friend, looking at my first attempts, said she loved my "folk art." Too bad that wasn't the art form I was struggling so hard to produce!

I would have been discouraged except for something I had read ina book on Chinese painting. The author mentioned that the traditional Chinese view of creativity was different than our American view. The typical American believes that you're either born with talent or you're consigned to the scrap heap of the "not artistic." The Chinese view is that the road to creativity begins with the patient practice of learning skills by copying the masters who have gone before you—in other words, first things first.

Well, of course I'm quintessentially American and I wanted to be immediately wonderful, but the depressing fact was that my early attempts were dreadful. Obviously, I wasn't going to get better without effort. I would have thrown the whole enterprise out, but,

alas, I had discovered the sheer joy of applying ink and paint to paper, and no matter how bad the results, I couldn't turn back.

It took some time for me to discover why I was so determined to proceed with what a more rational person would have deemed a fool's enterprise. It turns out that I love color. I love design. I love paints, brushes, inks, fabrics, papers, raffia, ribbons, buttons, and beads. When I work with these materials, cutting and pasting, drawing and painting, I lose track of my other life of schedules, lists, and duties. From the very beginning of my cardmaking attempts, I loved getting absorbed in the process. One doesn't have to be "artistic" to spend time and effort working in a chosen medium; one only has to sit down and do it.

Cards are the perfect medium for practicing with color and design. A card that isn't so wonderful will teach you what not to do, and you can deep-six it without the penalty of having spent a great deal of time on it. But a card that is wonderful will give you that feeling of glee you get when your creation turns out to be something better than you thought you could make. Keep it or share it. A great card is a little work of art.

about this book

When I teach a class, I bring a few of my cards with their corresponding templates. I bring a number of other cards for students to use as models or to stimulate design ideas. Then I demonstrate two or three very basic techniques.

Students use my templates to make their first card. Once they get that under their belt, they surprise themselves by abandoning the template technique. Working with one of my cards as a model, they draw and cut their next cards freehand. Soon after that, they decide my card designs need serious tweaking, and they enhance or change them in some way. By the end of the day, many are designing their own cards!

I love this process and have designed the book with this in mind. There are twelve cards with full-size templates; you might start with one of these. The remaining cards can be drawn and cut freehand using my cards as models, or the cards in the book can be copied for templates. Project instructions include enlargement percentages where necessary.

As a quilter, I have a large stash of fabric sitting idly around my workroom, and some years back I hit upon the idea of pasting fabric to paper, a hybrid I call "papric." This concoction can be cut up and used exactly like paper. Furthermore, by turning fabric into paper, I have on hand colors and designs I would never find in paper alone. Most of the cards in this book use papric because its texture and look appeal to me.

However, paper selections are much more interesting now than when I discovered this technique, so if you're not a "fabric" person and don't want to become one, almost all the card designs in the book can be made using paper instead of papric. If the supply list calls for "papric," just think "paper."

Read through the "Basic Supplies" and "Techniques" sections of the book before starting your first project. For each project, you will need the basic supplies as well as the specific project supplies. The project how-to instructions are very simple; however, they assume you have read through the "Techniques" section and have a good idea of what to do.

WE'RE THROWING A PARTY!

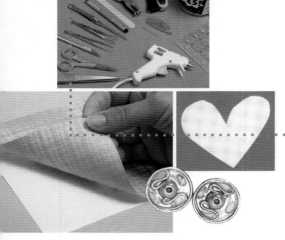

basic supplies

Cardmaking supplies are easy to find and inexpensive. Many of the supplies are available at art and craft stores. You will also find supplies at fabric stores, variety stores, stationery stores, and scrapbook stores.

Papers

Card Blanks

Cardmaking starts with a "card blank." This will be the background you decorate. For the card blank, use one of the following types of medium-weight to heavyweight paper:

- Card stock or cover-weight paper.

- Large sheets of colored papers. My favorite is Canson Mi-Teintes paper. When cut to card size, this folds easily and makes attractive blanks. These papers are also useful as a colored background on a white or cream-colored card blank and for the design elements pasted or glued to the cards.

- Watercolor paper. Since it won't actually be used for watercolor, buy the least expensive pad and cut the sheets to the size you need.

- Precut card blanks with matching envelopes. Often these cards have a deckled and colored edge. If you buy precut cards that are a different size than the project card, enlarge or decrease the size of the templates as needed.

Card Design Elements

For the card design elements, use lightweight to medium-weight paper and text paper:

- Handmade papers. These papers come in a variety of colors and weights.

- Text paper in fun colors and designs. Select paper with an overall design; the sort with borders is less useful.

- Corrugated paper. Although you can buy corrugated paper in some colors, you can make corrugated paper out of paper you already have on hand using a Fiskars corrugating tool.

Inserts

For a touch of elegance, I glue inserts in all my cards. This allows me to write a message on the insert and not on the card. For more on inserts, see "Using Inserts," page 16.

- Text-weight bond paper or computer printer paper.

Envelopes

An envelope should be $\frac{1}{4}''$ larger in height and width than the folded card. A card that is dimensional some-times requires a slightly larger envelope than a flat card would. If an envelope is more than $\frac{1}{4}''$ thick or exceeds the standard size or weight, extra postage should be added to it.

- Standard envelopes in a variety of colors and sizes. The projects in this book call for standard-sized envelopes.
- Handmade envelopes from your selection of papers.

Papers and envelopes

Fabrics

Fabric gives these cards a great look and texture.

- Fabrics in a range of colors and designs. If you don't have what quilters call a "stash," select two or three projects and buy ¼-yard cuts of the fabrics you'll need. If you do a number of the book projects, you'll soon have your "stash" of fabrics.
- Scraps. Many fabric stores sell small bags of scraps, and some fabric stores have bulletin boards for information and exchange; you could post your name and ask for scraps. If you know someone who quilts or sews, ask him or her for leftovers.
- Sequined and lamé fabrics. If you don't have these on hand, buy ¼ yard each.

···· **Tip** ·····························

Wash all but the sequined and lamé fabrics to remove the sizing. (Washing the fabric generally results in a certain amount of raveling. Save any raveled threads; they can be used on the cards later.)

Glues and Pastes

I use paste, glue, and rubber cement for different purposes.

- Paste. My favorite paste, a brand called Yes, is an archival-quality paste that can be thinned with water and works equally well with fabric and paper. When project instructions say "paste," this is the paste to use.
- Glue gun and glue sticks. Use a low-heat glue gun and glue sticks to fasten three-dimensional items such as beads, bows, feathers, and twigs. When project instructions say "glue," use the glue gun.
- Rubber cement. Use rubber cement to cement inserts into cards. When project instructions say "cement," use rubber cement instead of paste or glue.

Cutting Supplies

Good quality cutting supplies make the job easier and more successful.

- A rotary cutter, mat board, and clear rulers. If you don't have a mat board already, buy one that is at least 35″ × 23″. Anything smaller makes it difficult to cut up large sheets of paper. You will also need these tools for cutting fabric.
- 5″ Fiskars scissors (the style with the very sharp points) or equivalent. These are a must for cutting the small pieces you'll use in making cards.
- 8″ Fiskars scissors or equivalent for the larger cuts.
- Hole punch.
- X-acto or craft knife for scoring heavyweight papers.
- Optional: Paper cutter with an 18″ bed to cut card blanks.

···· **Tip** ·····························

I use double-sided tape to attach a piece of fine sandpaper to the back of my clear ruler to prevent slipping.

Miscellaneous Supplies

Keep your supplies handy.

- Permanent pens. A fine black felt-tip pen, such as a Pigma Micron pen, size .01.

- A good pair of needle-nose or bent-nose tweezers to make handling small pieces easy.

- Brayer for making papric.

- Reverse tweezers to hold threads and strings together while you work with them. Most projects don't require them; if I used this tool in making the project, I put it on the supply list for the project.

- A large needle such as a #18 tapestry needle. If you tie inserts into a card, this needle is big enough to put ribbon or tie through the fold of a card. Project instructions will call for this if needed.

- Tongue depressor to spread paste evenly.

- Fiskars corrugator for corrugating paper of any weight.

Gluing, cutting, and miscellaneous supplies

Craft Supplies

If you need these, the supply list for the card you're making will say so.

- "Pearls." These come on a string and can be cut into shorter lengths.

- Narrow bamboo sticks. If you can't get these, buy skewers from a kitchen store. To make a kitchen skewer look more like bamboo, take a Sharpie pen and ink in small $\frac{1}{16}''$-wide "nodes." These should be about $2''$ apart.

- Saw grass.

- Raffia.

- Beads in different colors and sizes.

- Narrow ribbons ($\frac{1}{8}''$–$\frac{1}{4}''$).

- Cork paper.

- Doilies.

- Stamens.

- Small flowers and leaves.

- A variety of sequins and metallic shapes such as musical notes, spokes, and so on.

- Aleene's Glitter Snow.

- Scribbles.

- Feathers.

- Stickers.

- Polyester stuffing. (Not shown.)

Craft supplies

Found Supplies

These supplies are free. I call this "direct recycling."

- Colored envelopes or flyers. Your mail can be a good source of colored paper. Cut out and use any unprinted areas. Often this paper is heavy enough that the reverse side will not show print.

- Commemorative cancelled stamps. To remove them from the envelope, see "Working with Stamps," page 15.

- Raveled threads. When you wash your fabrics, save the raveled thread. This makes wonderful hair and flowers.

- Leftover yarn and trim.

- Feathers for tying flies. If a friend or family member is a fisherman, he or she may have some. Filch a few.

- Packing foam. Many shipments include pieces of foam about $1/8''-1/4''$ thick. This foam is an ideal base for lifting designs up off the card. One piece of foam will make a lot of cards!

- An assortment of small beads.

Found supplies

Additional Found Supplies Not Shown in Photo

- Gold envelope liners. At holiday time, I often receive cards in envelopes that have lovely pieces of gold paper inside. I cut out this gold paper; it's wonderful for accents.

- Raffia bows. If someone gives you a gift with a raffia bow, save it.

- Buttons, hooks and eyes, tiny bells, bits of narrow wire, snaps, and broken jewelry that yields small beads or glass stones.

- Old cotton shirts. Pasting is a messy business, so cut up rags to keep your work and hands clean.

- Scrap paper and junk mail. Use as a pasting base. Do not use newspaper or magazines.

··· **Tip** ···············

These small found objects can often be used on cards. If you take a box and throw these things into it, they may ultimately lead you to a new card design.

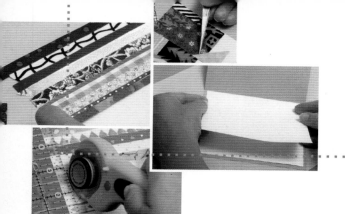

techniques

Scoring and Folding a Card Blank

"Scoring" is the process of indenting or cutting paper to ease the process of folding it into a card blank. Once a card blank is folded, you can use it horizontally or vertically. Project instructions give the size of the card before folding.

For heavy card stock, follow these steps:

1 Line up the card blank on the mat board. If you feel the paper has a "right" or "wrong" side, lay it right side up.

2 Use a clear ruler to gauge the halfway point of the card and run an X-acto knife lightly down the edge of the ruler—grazing, rather than cutting, the surface of the card. You will soon get the feel of how hard you must press to score the card correctly.

3 Fold the card with the indentation on the outside of the card blank.

Scoring the card

For medium-weight paper:

1 Simply fold the card blank in half, matching the corners and edges.

2 Press the fold with the back of a fingernail.

Cutting

Keep your cutting tools sharp. When cutting, make sure your scissors are at a 90° angle to the paper or fabric. This will give you the cleanest cut. Move the paper or fabric instead of the scissors.

···· Tip ·····························

Don't worry about dents or folds in the paper. Pasting will smooth these imperfections out.

Pasting and Gluing

Pasting

A good pasting technique will produce a satisfactory card that dries well. Have on hand 2 small rags (one damp and one dry), a tongue depressor to apply the paste, tweezers, and a lot of scrap paper to protect your working surface.

Yes paste takes a few minutes to dry. This is good because in many of the projects a card piece is pasted down and then partly pulled up to slip something else underneath it.

1 Start by laying the piece to be pasted on a piece of clean scrap paper.

2 Use a tongue depressor to apply the paste, holding the long edge of the tongue depressor at a slight angle to the piece you're pasting.

3 Start from the middle of the piece and work outward. Extend the paste beyond the edges and onto the scrap paper. This will ensure that the edges are completely covered.

4 Look at the pasted piece at an angle that reflects light to check for areas that you might have missed. The pasted area will appear shiny and any dry areas will be noticeable. Apply paste to any dry areas.

Applying paste

5 Don't use too much paste. This will make the piece thick and create drying difficulties. To ensure that you don't have too much paste, take the long edge of the tongue depressor and scrape it over the piece, removing any excess. Put the leftover paste back in the jar.

Removing excess paste

6 If you've done this correctly, you'll probably have a bit of paste on your hands. Clean them up with the damp rag.

When pasting card design elements, pick up the pasted piece with tweezers and lay it in place on your card. Blot the edges of the pasted piece with a dry rag (don't rub). This will take up any excess paste.

···· Tip ·····································

To paste very tiny pieces, smear a small dab of paste on scrap paper. Use tweezers to pick up each small piece and drag it lightly over the paste. Press it to the card and blot with a damp or dry rag.

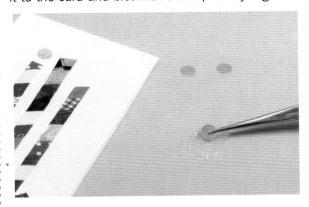

Pasting small pieces using tweezers

Gluing

To use a glue gun, follow these steps:

1 Heat the gun for 10 minutes.

2 Use tweezers to pick up and hold the design elements while you carefully apply small amounts of glue to them.

3 Gently press the pieces into place on the project.

A low-heat glue gun makes "strings." When they dry, pull them off the card, ball them up, and discard them. Don't "fiddle" with drying glue; it won't dry clear if you touch it before it has dried. If you've applied too much glue, you can try to take up any excess with a craft knife, but be aware that it's all too easy to make things worse instead of better!

Making Papric

Papric is a hybrid of fabric pasted to paper, which when dry, can be cut up and used as card backgrounds and card design elements.

In this book, I describe the basic method of making single-fabric papric and its three variations: striped, "woven," and patchwork papric. You can use any text paper for the paper base to make papric. Use old writing tablets or computer paper. A 5″ × 5″ square works for any background or card detail in this book.

Single-Fabric Papric (METHOD 1)

When a project simply calls for papric, I am referring to single-fabric papric (Method 1).

1 Cut a 5″ × 5″ piece of paper for a base and a 5″ × 5″ piece of fabric. If you have an odd-shaped fabric scrap that you want to make into papric, put it on a sheet of paper and cut the paper base to the fabric shape.

2 Apply Yes paste to the paper base using the technique on page 11. Place the fabric right side up on the base and gently press it into the paste.

3 Turn the pasted piece fabric side down on a clean piece of scrap paper and use a damp rag to press the paper base into the fabric. The damp rag wets the paper slightly, ensuring better adhesion. Be careful to press, not rub. Roll a brayer over the paper base from the center out—rather like making piecrust.

4 Set the papric aside to dry before you attempt to cut it. Sometimes the papric curls as it dries; this won't affect its future use.

Striped Papric (METHOD 2)

To make an interesting piece of papric, cut bias strips of varying widths (¼″ to ½″) from your fabric scraps and paste them to the base paper to create stripes. Cut sequined fabrics on the straight of grain.

1 Cut a 5″ × 5″ piece of paper for a base.

2 Use a rotary cutter, mat board, and ruler to cut fabric strips. The strips should be cut evenly, a minimum of 5″ long. If the strip is longer, don't bother to trim it. Accumulate all the strips you will need before starting.

3 Apply paste to the base. Starting at the top, lay the first strip on, using tweezers to gently press the fabric into the paste.

···· Tip ····

Substitute a ⅛″ to ½″ ribbon for a fabric strip. This makes a great accent.

4 Butt the next strip up against the first strip. Be careful not to overlap strips. Press each piece into place. Continue this process, varying the colors and widths of the fabric strips.

5 When the base is covered, go to Steps 3–4 in "Single-Fabric Papric," at left.

···· Tip ····

If the paste starts to dry before you've finished, simply reapply paste below the area you've already worked and continue on.

Making single-fabric papric

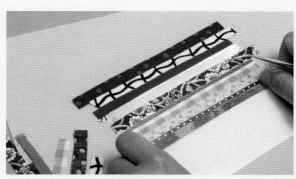

Making striped papric

"Woven" Papric (METHOD 3)

This papric looks complex but isn't. Your friends and relatives will think you cut up dozens of tiny squares and tediously glued them together to make this card.

1 Make a 5″ × 5″ piece of striped papric (Method 2) using ⅜″ bias strips. When the papric is dry, square up the piece with a rotary cutter. Lay the piece in front of you with the stripes vertical.

2 Make ⅜″ horizontal cuts across the papric.

3 Cut a 5″ × 5″ piece of paper for a base and apply paste to it.

4 Start at the top of the base and set a strip into the paste. Take the next strip, offset the squares by one, and set the strip into the paste. Continue (alternating back and forth) until the strips are all pasted.

5 Let the "woven" papric dry before cutting it.

···· **Tip** ·································

Make a different-looking woven papric by cutting each strip into 2 or 3 pieces of random lengths. Mix up all these strips and paste them to the base.

Making "woven" papric

Pasting strips onto paper base

Patchwork Papric (METHOD 4)

Any shape with a 45°, 90°, or 135° angle can be used to make a patchwork design. These shapes include squares, rectangles, 45° parallelograms, and right triangles.

1 Cut a 5″ × 5″ piece of text paper for a base.

2 Cut squares from a variety of fabrics. These squares can be any size from ½″ to 2½″.

3 Cut the larger squares diagonally to make right triangles. You can cut the larger right triangles in half to make even smaller triangles.

4 Cut rectangles no smaller than ½″ × ¾″ and no larger than 1″ × 1½″.

5 Apply paste to the base. Start at a top corner and set a square or rectangular piece into the paste. Pick a different-size piece of any shape and butt it against the first piece. Don't overlap edges.

6 Use different-size pieces, fitting them into the angles and beside each other. Eventually, you will fit most of the pieces together. You may occasionally have to slightly trim a piece or manipulate the fabric by "shrinking" or stretching it.

7 When the base is covered, go to Steps 3–4 in "Single-Fabric Papric," page 12.

Making patchwork papric

···· **Tip** ·································

I keep a stash of papric around so that when I want to make a card, it is available quickly.

Making a Deckled Edge on Paper

Deckled edges are torn or unfinished edges. Deckling works best on handmade or lightweight papers.

1 Measure your paper to determine the size card you want and make a fold where you want the deckle to be.

2 Wet a small paintbrush and brush water across the fold.

3 Let the water penetrate the paper fiber. Gently tear the paper along the fold.

···· **Tip** ·································

If you are deckling an already cut edge, brush water along the edge of the paper. When the paper seems soaked, hold the edge between your thumb and index finger and gently pull.

Using Templates

1 Many of the projects in this book do not have templates; these are projects with simple design elements that can be drawn and cut freehand. Remember, whimsy is the order of the day. A card needn't be perfect or symmetrical.

2 If you have trouble drawing and cutting freehand, you can make templates by copying the card picture. Project instructions include enlargement percentages if necessary. Cut the card elements out of the copied cards and use these as templates.

3 There are 12 projects with full size templates. To use them, trace or make a copy of them and cut them out. Reverse them on the back of the paper or papric, pencil around them, and cut out the design. Transfer any markings.

···· **Tip** ·································

When I buy an instruction book I take it to a copy store, have the binding cut off, and have the book spiral bound. This allows me to trace or copy patterns easily.

Creating Quotes and Messages

I often hear people say, "I don't know what to write on the inside of a blank card." All that white space seems intimidating.

I recall an old Vermont adage: "Talk less, say more." Having gone to the trouble of making a friend a handmade card, what else needs to be said? I simply write, "Dear ..., Happy Birthday! Love, Susan." I write large, center the message in the middle of the insert, add a date at the end, and I'm done.

If I incorporate what might be an inside message (such as "Happy Birthday") into the outside card design, I write, "Dear ..., Have a great year. Love, Susan." No one has ever complained to me about this brevity.

It's not as if I have nothing to say. I feel free to spread my opinion around through the medium of quotes and adages, incorporating them into card designs. By doing this, I amuse my friends and relatives without having to think up anything at all original!

···· **Tip** ·································

When quotes are used, choose a larger size print for the quote and a smaller size for the author's name.

Getting It on the Card

To place your message on the card, follow these steps:

1 Print the quote or message. Cut it out with a small margin all around.

2 The size of the message should fit the card design. If the project calls for a message frame, check the size of the printed message against the frame. If there is no message frame, lay the printed message against the card to check the fit. If the message is too big or too small, adjust the font size and reprint it.

3 When you are satisfied with the fit, either paste the message directly to the card (where applicable) or paste it to the frame and paste the frame to the card.

Working with Packing Foam and Polyester Stuffing

Many cards are now made with a three-dimensional look. To get this look, I use packing foam or polyester stuffing.

1 To raise a card detail completely above the background, glue a small piece of packing foam to the back of the cut detail and then glue the foam only to the card. See "Little Sailboat," page 59.

Or . . .

2 To get a rounded or "plump" look in a card detail, glue a small piece of polyester stuffing to the center back of the detail. Then put glue around the edges of the detail. Glue to the card. See "Hen and Chicks," page 21.

Working with Stamps

Some projects call for postage stamps. To prepare cancelled stamps, follow these steps:

1 To remove the paper and backing from stamps, soak them in water for 30 minutes. The backing and glue should pull off easily; if they don't, leave the stamp in the water longer.

2 Dry the stamp before using it. Don't worry if it curls up; it will lie out flat again when you paste it.

Working with Feathers

Feathers come in different sizes. If you can't find really small feathers (1½″ to 2″ in size), you can cut larger feathers to the size you need. To use this technique, don't buy feathers more than 5″ long.

1 Cut 2″ off the top of the feather. Save this piece and discard the bottom.

2 Trim the feathers away from the bottom ¼″ of the feather shaft.

3 If the feather seems too wide for the length of the shaft, trim both sides down.

Trimming feathers

Cutting Greenery

Making "fir" branches for the "Mortarboard" card or "Birdhouse" card is not as hard as it looks. It's just a matter of snipping. These branches also look cute on a Christmas card.

1 Cut pieces of green paper or papric using the templates given.

2 Cut fairly vertical notches out of the bottom of the branch.

3 For the top of the branch, cut notches that are almost horizontal.

4 Position these branches on the card until you have a natural look, with some branches longer and some shorter. If any part of the branch is wider than the card, trim it.

Snipping branches

Making Raveled Thread Flowers

To make the raveled thread flower, take 7–10 raveled threads about 1˝ long and double them into a U shape. Glue the bottom of the U down and flare the top of the flower out. You can also make these flowers by cutting thread off a spool. Trim the tops of them.

Working with Scribbles

Scribbles is a fabric and paper paint that comes in a little bottle with an applicator tip. To use Scribbles, follow these steps:

1 To prime the bottle, place the tip of the bottle on a piece of scrap paper. Squeeze the bottle to start the paint flow.

2 Use the applicator tip to apply the paint, squeezing the bottle with an even pressure while moving it.

3 After painting, don't touch the painted piece for at least 4 hours.

Finishing a Card

Drying

After the application of glue, paste, paint, or ink, cards need to be dried carefully.

1 Dry your card flat to prevent distortion. Sometimes the front of a card becomes concave. If this happens, push the card front out into a convex shape.

Or . . .

2 You may also press your card to dry it, as long as the card design is not three-dimensional. To press the card, put pieces of scrap paper over and under it. Lay the card under some heavy books. Check your card after 15–20 minutes to make sure it's drying correctly.

Occasionally cards dried by pressing turn up very slightly at the open corners. This is usually because the card was somewhat more dimensional than it seemed to be.

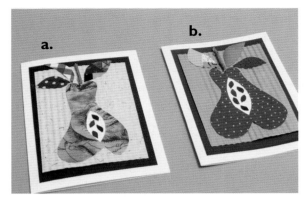

a. Card dried correctly; b. Card dried incorrectly

Signing Your Card

A card is a little work of art and worth signing. Study the card design to determine where to sign your card. Occasionally, I sign along the side of a stem or some other design on the card. Use a fine-tip pen for your signature.

Using Inserts

Card projects specify an insert size. I usually write out my message on the card insert before I cement it into the card. If you're making announcements, print or copy the announcement, cut the insert to the size needed, and then cement or tie it in.

Cementing an Insert into the Card

1 Cut and fold the insert in half. Run a line of rubber cement along the fold on the inside card front.

2 Fit the card fold and the insert fold together, centering the insert between the top and bottom of the card. Let dry.

Cementing the insert

Tying Inserts

1 Measure the fold and divide by 3. For example, a card with a 7″ fold divided by 3 = 2⅓″. Round this measurement down to something you can actually measure, in this case, 2¼″.

2 On the outside fold, measure 2¼″ in from both edges and make small dots with a pencil. The measurement between these dots, in the center of the fold, should be 2½″. The pencil dots are your punch guides.

3 Fold the insert and center it inside the card, matching the folds. Punch a tapestry needle through the dot on the outside fold and through the insert fold underneath. Pull the needle through the hole. Repeat for the other side.

4 Thread the needle with the tie. Run the tie through the hole to the inside of the card and back to the outside. Make a bow or a knot in the tie.

Tying the insert

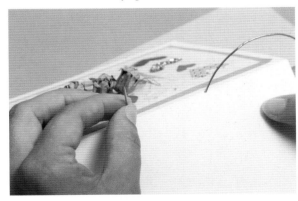

Duplicating Cards

Once you've made a card by hand, you have an alternative to remaking it. By scanning a card to a computer file, you can print as many cards as you like on card paper. It's not handmade, but it's close.

Printing Postcards

Some invitations, moving notices, and even baby announcements can be sent as postcards. Postcards made this way will be 4¼″ × 5½″.

1 Set up a word-processing file to print the announcement information on what will be the back of the postcard. Format 4 of these prints to a page, remembering to allow space for an address. Print on 8½″ × 11″ card stock.

2 Scan the handmade card into the computer and adjust the size of the card to a 4″ × 5¼″ format. To do this, you may need software that allows you to change the ratio proportions of the card.

3 Print the scanned and adjusted image 4 to a page on the other side of the card stock. Cut the postcards out and mail them.

Printing Cards

You can print a card in one of two ways:

1 Scan the card. Print it in the upper right page position, then score and fold it. Cut it to size.

OR

2 Slightly reduce the size of the card, print the scanned card to text paper, cut the design out, and paste it to a precut, prefolded card blank cut to the original card size. Use a different color card stock than the original card background.

Duplicating a card

Supplies

- A 10″ × 7″ card blank and a 9½″ × 6½″ insert, both folded.

- A 4″ × 5½″ paper background, pasted to the front of the card.

- Small bits of papric in 5 or 6 different greens for shamrocks.

- A cream colored papric for flowers.

- Stamens.

Before starting, read "Techniques," pages 10–17.

Draw the templates freehand or copy the card, enlarging it by 125%, and cut the templates out.

How-To

1 Cut out the shamrock leaves and paste them to the card.

2 Cut the shamrock flowers out of the cream papric and paste them to the card. Pick up the bottom edge of the flower and stick a few stamens underneath. Press it down again.

3 With a black pen, draw stems for the flowers and shamrock leaves.

4 Put several strokes at the base of the stems to simulate grass. Draw grass as it grows, from the bottom up.

Luck never gives, it only lends.
—Swedish proverb

Before starting, read "Techniques," pages 10–17.

Supplies

- A 10″ × 7″ card blank and a 9½″ × 6½″ insert, both folded.

- A 4″ × 6″ background of papric or paper that looks like forest or woodland, pasted to the front of the card.

- Raffia, stamens, twigs from your yard, and some small leaves from the craft store.

- An 8″ × ¹⁄₁₆″ strip of heavy black paper.

How-To

1 Twist the strip of black paper about halfway around. Do this every ½″ or so to make it bend and look like it has nodes in it. Cut it up into 2″–3″ lengths to use as a dark weed.

2 Glue on the black paper weeds, twigs, stamens, raffia, and small leaves.

3 Add a grasshopper if you have a bit of watercolor paint; however, the card works just as well without a bug.

Before starting, read "Techniques," pages 10–17.

Draw the templates freehand or copy the card, enlarging it by 125%, and cut the templates out.

Supplies

- A 10″ × 7″ card blank and a 9½″ × 6½″ insert, both folded.

- Leftover paprics and papers for hearts and frames.

- Two ¼″ × 4½″ strips and two ¼″ × 6½″ strips of paper or papric for the grid.

How-To

1 Cut out the background frames and hearts, and position them on the card.

2 Intertwine the paper strips.

3 When you are satisfied with the placement, paste everything down.

*A good heart is better than
all the heads in the world.*

—E. Bulwer-Lytton

Before starting, read "Techniques," pages 10–17.

Draw the templates freehand or copy the card, enlarging it by 125%, and cut the templates out.

Supplies

■ A 10″ × 7″ card blank and a 9½″ × 6½″ insert, both folded.

■ A piece of papric for the hen and chicks.

■ Trim or feathers for the hen's tail.

■ Red felt or papric for the hen's crown.

■ Orange paper for the beaks.

■ 3 small black beads for the chicks' eyes and 1 larger black bead for the hen's eye.

■ Stamens.

■ Polyester stuffing.

How-To

1 Cut out the hen and 3 chicks. (Two chicks face right and one faces left.) Cut out the hen's crown. Cut 1 larger and 3 smaller triangles from the orange paper for the beaks.

2 Glue a small amount of stuffing to the center back of the hen. Glue the edges of the hen to the card.

3 Paste the chicks and the beaks. Glue the hen's crown in place.

4 Use a black pen to draw the legs and feet. Glue the stamens around the feet.

5 Glue on the beads for the eyes.

6 Cut the amount of trim needed for the hen's tail feathers and glue into place.

Supplies

- An 8½″ × 5½″ card blank and an 8″ × 5″ insert, both folded.

- A 3″ × 4″ background of papric or paper, pasted to the card front.

- A small piece of orange papric for the large flower.

- Raveled threads for the smaller flowers.

- 4 tiny glass beads for the large flower center.

- Green papric and paper for leaves and stems.

- A 2″ × 2″ square each of white and yellow corrugated paper and a 2″ × 2″ square of text paper for the basket.

Before starting, read "Techniques," pages 10–17.

Draw the templates freehand or copy the card, enlarging it by 115%, and cut the templates out.

How-To

1 See Steps 1–3 in "Baby Buggy" page 44, for instructions on weaving the basket.

2 Cut the basket down to a 1¾″ × 1⅞″ square. Reglue the ends of the strips if necessary. Paste the basket to the card.

3 Cut some long leaves out of the green papric and a very narrow long stem for the large flower. Paste these in place, slipping them under the top of the basket.

4 To make the large flower, cut 6 small pointed oval shapes out of the orange papric and paste them in

place to look like an open flower. Glue the beads in the center.

5 Make 5 raveled thread flowers.

6 Use a fine-tip felt pen to draw stems on these flowers. Cut tiny leaves out of the green paper to paste around the stems.

Before starting, read "Techniques,"
pages 10–17.

Draw the templates freehand or
copy the templates on page 77.

Supplies

For either card:

- An 8½″ × 5½″ card blank and an 8″ × 5″ insert, both folded.

- A piece of papric for the cradle.

- A 2″ × 3″ piece of paper for the rocker.

- A 1½″ × 2″ piece of fabric for the blanket.

- A #18 tapestry needle.

- A 1½″ × 3½″ message frame.

- Metallic musical notes (for the blue card).

- 10″ of ribbon or yarn for ties.

How-To

1 Ravel the 2 long edges and 1 short edge of the blanket fabric.

2 Cut the rocker out and paste it to the card.

3 Cut the cradle out of the papric and paste it on top of the rocker.

4 Lift up the top of the cradle bed and fold the blanket under and over the top of it, putting the unraveled edge under the cradle. Press the cradle down. You may need to add more paste.

5 Print, frame, and paste one of the quotes.

6 Glue down the edges of the blanket and paste the musical notes.

···· **Tip** ·······················

When I am invited to a wedding, I substitute a small card like this for the response card that comes with the invitation. I write the correct formal acceptance on the inside of my card and send it back in the stamped envelope I received. This provides some diversion for the distraught bride and her harried mother.

Before starting, read "Techniques," pages 10–17.

Draw the templates freehand or copy the card and cut the templates out.

Supplies

- A 6½″ × 5″ card blank and a 6″ × 4½″ insert, both folded.

- Cancelled stamps for the books.

- Black paper cut into two ⅛″ × 4¾″ strips, two ⅛″ × 3¼″ strips, and one ⅛″ × 2¼″ strip for the bookshelf.

- Fine-tip colored pens to draw the flowers, a bit of papric or a cancelled stamp for the vase, and glass beads for the flower centers.

How-To

1 Glue the black strips to the card as shown. Trim the edges, if necessary.

2 Cut out the names or themes of the stamps to make little books. Paste them to the card.

3 Cut out the vase and paste it to the card. With the colored pens, draw in stems, leaves, and flowers. Glue a tiny bead to the center of each flower.

We are what we repeatedly do. Excellence, then, is not an act, but a habit.

—Aristotle

How to Write a Response Card

I often write out a response card to an invitation other than a wedding. I've been asked, why write a card? Why not phone? You mean, besides the fact that I'm a curmudgeon?

There is a reason to write a card. If I want to decline an invitation, talking to someone on the phone almost requires that I give some excuse, whether or not I have one. It's very difficult to call a person and say, "I'm not coming. Good-bye." But if I send a response card instead of phoning, I can accept or decline in style, and no excuses are necessary.

Here's the form. It's supposed to be handwritten, but we all make compromises.

Ms. Susan S. Terry

accepts with pleasure

the kind invitation of

Ms. Amanda Gurr

for Thursday

the third of September.

Ms. Susan S. Terry

regrets that she is

unable to accept

the very kind invitation of

Ms. Christina Doak

for Sunday

the twenty-ninth of January.

Write or print out the message, cut the page to fit inside the response card, cement it in, and mail it. You'd spend twenty minutes phoning anyway.

Supplies

- A 9″ × 6¼″ card blank made from watercolor paper, folded. Cut an additional ¼″ off the bottom of the front of the card.

- A 3″ × 3″ square of blue paper or papric for the background, pasted to the card front.

- Gold papric and gold paper for bells.

- 2 punch holes of gold metallic paper or 2 beads for the clappers.

- 6″ of ⅛″ gold ribbon for the bows on the bells.

- 10″ of gold tie for the bow at the top of the card.

- An 8″ × 5¾″ insert.

- A #18 tapestry needle.

Before starting, read "Techniques," pages 10–17.

Draw the templates freehand or copy the card, enlarging it by 120%, and cut the templates out.

How-To

1 Cut and paste the bells and clappers to the blue background.

2 Cut 6″ of gold ribbon, make a small bow, and glue it to the top of the bells.

3 For the insert, plan the invitation format for a 4″ × 5¾″ space to be printed on the bottom half of the page. This space includes margins, so the actual print layout will be smaller.

4 Once the insert is printed, fold and tie it into the card.

Supplies

- A 10″ × 7″ card blank and a 9½″ × 6½″ insert, both folded.

- Text paper.

- A 4¾″ × 1⅛″ piece of paper or papric and a white doily for the tablecloths.

- 5 birthday candles.

- Dark brown papric or paper for the cake.

- Textured handmade white paper for the icing.

- 5 punch holes from metallic gold paper for the flames. (The flames can also be painted on with Scribbles.)

Before starting, read "Techniques," pages 10–17.

Draw the templates freehand or copy the card, enlarging it by 125%, and cut the templates out.

How-To

1 Type out a sequence of phrases ("happy birthday to you" and "happy birthday happy birthday") until you fill a page. Print to text paper. Let the page dry and cut it down to 4¾″ × 6″. Paste it to the card.

2 Paste the tablecloth to the bottom of the card. Cut the doily to fit the tablecloth and paste it on.

3 Cut out the cake and icing layers and paste them on.

4 Use an X-acto knife to slit the candles lengthwise. Cut the bottoms off to shorten them, and glue them on top of the cake, flat side down.

5 Glue the gold punch holes to the tops of the candles.

Susan Terry

Supplies

- A 10″ × 7″ card blank and a 9½″ × 6½″ insert, both folded.

- A 4½″ × ³⁄₁₆″ piece of paper and two ¼″ square pieces for the rod and finials.

- A 4″ × 5¼″ piece of paper or papric for the banner.

- Leftover pieces of papric or paper for the gifts.

- Thread and ⅛″–¼″ ribbons for the bows.

- ⅛″ strips of colored paper snipped into tiny pieces for confetti.

- A 2″ × ⅝″ message frame.

Before starting, read "Techniques," pages 10–17.

Draw the templates freehand or copy the card, enlarging it by 125%, and cut the templates out.

How-To

1 Cut scallops on the bottom of the banner piece or use pinking shears to make a cute edge. Cut six ¼″ × ⅝″ rectangles out of the top of the banner, which will leave 7 loops to "hang" on the rod.

2 Paste the rod, finials, and banner to the card.

3 Cut out the gifts and paste them to the banner.

4 Make the bows and glue them to the card.

5 Paste on the confetti pieces.

6 Print the message; frame it and paste it to the card.

Tip

I like banner cards because they're versatile. Put balloons or a cake on a banner for a birthday card; put eggs on a banner for an Easter card; put holly or candy canes on a banner for a Christmas card.

Supplies

For either card:

- A 9″ × 6¼″ card blank and an 8½″ × 5¾″ insert, both folded.

- A 3⅞″ × 5½″ piece of corrugated white paper, glued to the card blank.

- A 5″ × 5″ square of patchwork papric (Method 4) done in pinks or blues for the dress or overalls.

- 2 small buttons or beads for the shoulder buttons.

- 6″ of ⅛″ pink ribbon for the bow (dress).

Before starting, read "Techniques," pages 10–17.

Draw the templates freehand or copy the card, enlarging it by 120% for dress and 150% for overalls, and cut the templates out.

How-To

1 Cut the dress or overalls out of the patchwork papric.

2 Paste the dress or overalls to the corrugated background.

3 Glue the beads or buttons into place on the shoulders.

4 For the dress, tie a small pink bow and glue it on. Trim to shape.

Supplies

- An 8½″ × 5½″ card blank and an 8″ × 5″ insert, both folded.

- A 4″ × 5″ piece of papric, pasted to the card front.

- A 1½″ × 2″ piece of papric for the lampshade and a tiny piece of paper for the base.

- A button for the lamp finial and small beads for the pull.

- A feather and tiny piece of black paper for the quill and inkwell.

- A Sharpie Fine-Point pen.

- A 1″ × 1½″ message frame and a tiny paper heart.

Before starting, read "Techniques," pages 10–17.

Draw the templates freehand or copy the card, enlarging it by 115%, and cut the templates out.

How-To

1 With a pencil, lightly draw the lamp directly on the papric. This doesn't have to be a perfect shape. Go over the pencil line with the Sharpie.

2 Paste the shade on the lamp. Cut out the lamp base and paste it on.

3 Cut out the inkwell and cut a feather down for the quill. Paste the inkwell to the card, with the tip of the quill under it.

4 Print the message and paste the heart below it; frame the message and paste it to the card. With the Pigma pen, draw the picture wire on the background.

5 Glue on the lamp finial. Glue on the beads for the lamp pull.

··· **Thank You Note Tips** ·······

A thank you note doesn't need to be long and doesn't need to be creative, but it does need to be mailed. Write the gift giver's full name and address on an envelope. Find a stamp and stick it on. When you have the envelope ready, you are more likely to send the note.

Supplies

- A 10″ × 7″ card blank and a 9½″ × 6½″ insert, both folded.

- A 4½″ × ⅜″ piece of papric for the windowsill.

- A 3⅞″ × 3½″ piece of blue papric for the sky.

- A 4″ × 2¼″ piece of papric for the window shade.

- A piece of mottled rusty-colored papric for the pot. Or use cork paper.

- 4¼″ of trim for the bottom of the shade.

- Wired leaves or small craft flowers for the plant.

Before starting, read "Techniques," pages 10–17.

Draw the templates freehand or copy the card, enlarging it by 125%, and cut the templates out.

How-To

1 Paste the windowsill, sky, and shade to the card, butting the pieces against each other.

2 Cut out and paste the flowerpot to the card.

3 Glue the wired leaves or flowers in place, sticking the ends under the pot.

4 Glue down the edging trim for the shade. Trim to fit or turn the edges under.

*Always do right.
This will gratify some people
and astonish the rest.*
—Mark Twain

O'er the land
of the free....

Susan Terrur

Supplies

- A 10″ × 7″ card blank and a 9½″ × 6½″ insert, both folded.

- A piece of red-and-white-striped papric (Method 2) for the flag. For this, cut 8¼″ bias strips in red and 7¼″ bias strips in white. Start with a red strip.

- A 6″ length of bamboo for the flagpole and a bead for the top.

- Wired greenery.

- 2″ of gold thread.

- Small star stickers.

Before starting, read "Techniques," pages 10–17.

Draw the templates freehand or copy the templates on page 76.

Labor to keep alive in your heart that little spark of celestial fire called conscience.

—George Washington

How-To

1 Wrap the gold thread once around the flagpole and glue both ends of the pole to the card. The pole should be slightly angled. Glue the bead on top of the pole.

2 Cut out the flag and paste it to the card in template order (a–d).

3 Work the gold thread into position and put it under the bottom of the flag.

4 Cut a few pieces of the wired greenery and glue them around the bottom of the pole. Stick the stars on the flag.

5 Print and paste the quote to the card.

Before starting, read "Techniques," pages 10–17.

Draw the templates freehand or copy the card, enlarging it by 125%, and cut the templates out.

Supplies

- A 10″ × 7″ card blank and a 9½″ × 6½″ insert, both folded.

- A 4½″ × 6″ background, pasted to the front of the card.

- 6 different sequined and/or lamé paprics for the ship and sails.

- Scribbles Iridescent Gold.

How-To

1 Cut the sails out of the papric and then paste the pieces to the card in this order: the ship, the 5 sails from right to left, and then the top 2 sails.

2 Use Scribbles paint to make a flag at the top of the sail. Let dry 4 hours.

Tip

Make this card in red, white, and blue and use it for a July birthday.

Before starting, read "Techniques," pages 10–17.

Draw the templates freehand or copy the card, enlarging it by 125%, and cut the templates out.

Supplies

- A 10″ × 7″ card blank and a 9½″ × 6½″ insert, both folded.

- A 4¼″ × 6″ background, pasted to the card front.

- A piece of patchwork papric (Method 4) for the fan.

- A piece of papric for the arched fan base.

- A 12″ length of ⅛″ ribbon.

How-To

1 Cut 8 fan blades from the papric.

2 Paste the 8 blades to the card. You may have to narrow the bottom or overlap them so the fan doesn't get too wide.

3 Cut an arched piece out of papric. This should cover the bottom of the fan blades.

4 Loop the ribbon 3 times. Glue the ribbon loops to the center back of the arched piece.

5 Glue the arched piece to the bottom of the fan blades.

Supplies

- A 10″ × 7″ card blank and a 9½″ × 6½″ insert, both folded.

- A 4½″ × 6½″ piece of papric for a background, pasted to the card front.

- Red papric for the flowers and some small beads for the centers.

- Green papric for the leaves.

- A 2¼″ × ⅞″ piece of sequined papric or metallic paper for the vase.

- Two 2½″ pieces of dark green raffia for the stems.

- A 2⅝″ × 3¼″ message frame.

· ·

Before starting, read "Techniques," pages 10–17.

Draw the templates freehand or copy the card, enlarging it by 125%, and cut the templates out.

· ·

> It is easier for a man to be loyal to his club than to his planet; the bylaws are shorter, and he is personally acquainted with the other members.
>
> Elwyn White.

The only way to have a friend is to be one.

—Ralph Waldo Emerson

How-To

1 Print the quote; frame it and paste it to the card.

2 Cut out the leaves and flower petals. Arrange the vase and leaves and paste them to the card. Arrange and slip the 2 stems under the vase.

3 Paste the flower petals in place and glue the beads to the flower centers.

what is this life,

if, full of care,

we have no time

to stand

and stare?

W.H. Davies

Supplies

- A 10″ × 7″ piece of card paper and a 9½″ × 6½″ insert, both folded.

- A piece of papric for the umbrella.

- A 5¼″ length of narrow bamboo for the umbrella post.

- Blue papric or paper for the waves.

- Papric made from terry cloth for the beach towel.

- Small glass beads for the sand.

- A piece of corrugated paper and a piece of black paper for the pail and shovel handle.

- Polyester stuffing for the clouds.

- A 1¾″ × 1½″ message frame (left) and a 1⅜″ × 1½″ frame (right).

How-To

1 Print the quote in 2 sections; frame it and paste it to the card.

2 Glue a thin layer of the polyester stuffing between the message frames for clouds.

3 Cut out the waves and paste them to the card.

4 Cut out the shovel handle, pail, and beach towel. Paste them to the card.

5 Cut out the umbrella and run a line of glue down the center back of it. Stick the bamboo into the glue,

Before starting, read "Techniques," pages 10–17.

Draw the templates freehand or copy the card, enlarging it by 125%, and cut the templates out.

leaving ½″ of bamboo above the umbrella. Glue the bamboo stick to the card. Glue down both sides of the umbrella, leaving the bottom free.

6 Glue beads to the card to simulate sand and add the birds.

Before starting, read "Techniques," pages 10–17.

Draw the templates freehand or copy the templates on page 76.

Supplies

- A 9″ × 6¼″ card blank and an 8½″ × 5¾″ insert, both folded.

- 2 paprics for the shirt and tie. I made papric from an old tie for the tie on this card.

- A 2½″ × ⅝″ piece of black paper and a 3″ × 1″ piece of white corrugated paper for the message frames.

How-To

1 Cut the shirt and right and left collar pieces out of one papric. Cut the tie and tie knot out of the other. Paste the shirt body, tie, tie knot, and two collar pieces on the card in that order. Be sure to match the X's on the collar when pasting. Check template.

2 Print the message; frame it and paste it to the card.

Before starting, read "Techniques," pages 10–17.

Draw the templates freehand or copy the card, enlarging it by 115%, and cut the templates out.

Supplies

- An 8½″ × 5½″ card blank and an 8″ × 5″ insert, both folded.

- A 5″ × 5″ square of "woven" papric (Method 3) for the basket.

- A piece of raffia for the basket handle.

- A 10″ piece of white ⅛″ ribbon for the bow.

- "Grass"—the kind you put in an Easter basket.

How-To

1 Cut the basket out of the "woven" papric and paste it to the card.

2 Cut an 8″ piece of raffia and arrange it on the card as a basket handle, slipping the ends under the basket.

3 Tie the ribbon into a bow and intertwine it with the raffia basket handle. Glue the bow and handle down.

4 Glue a small amount of grass in place.

Before starting, read "Techniques," pages 10–17.

Draw the templates freehand or copy the card, enlarging it by 120%, and cut the templates out.

Supplies

- A 9″ × 6¼″ card blank and an 8½″ × 5¾″ insert, both folded. I made my card blank from handmade paper.

- 2 pieces of papric made from sequined fabrics, a 5″ × 5″ square of striped papric (Method 2), and a piece of purple paper or papric.

- Tinsel-style Easter grass.

- Scribbles Iridescent Gold.

How-To

1 Cut 1 small egg out of the purple paper or papric. Use the Scribbles paints to paint wavy lines on this egg. Let dry 4 hours.

2 Cut 1 large egg and 1 small egg from the 2 sequined paprics.

3 Cut 2 small eggs from the striped papric, 1 with vertical stripes and 1 with diagonal stripes.

4 When the purple egg is dry, arrange the 5 eggs on the card. When you are satisfied with the placement, paste them down.

5 Glue down the grass.

6 Print the message and paste it to the card.

It's a boy!

S.Terry

Tip

If you know what gender your little lamb will be, make this card as an announcement. Whip up the cards ahead of the big event and address the envelopes. Once the baby arrives, print the vital info to 9½″ × 6½″ inserts, cement them in, and send the cards out.

Before starting, read "Techniques," pages 10–17.

Draw the templates freehand or copy the templates on page 77.

Supplies

- A 10″ × 7″ card blank in pale blue and a 9½″ × 6½″ insert, folded.

- A paper base for the lamb, made using the body template. Bias cut 35 strips ½″ × 2½″ from blue-and-white plaid fabric.

- A 4″ × 4″ piece of black paper for the legs and tail.

- A 3″ × 3″ piece of corrugated black paper for the head and ears.

- 2 beads for the eyes.

- A small jingle bell on a 2½″ piece of ⅛″ gold ribbon.

- A 1⅞″ × 1¼″ message frame.

How-To

1 Tie a knot in the center of each strip of the blue-and-white plaid strip. Start at the center of the lamb's body base and glue the knots, working outward and intertwining the fabric. Do this until the lamb looks woolly.

2 Cut out a tail. Cut 3 strips ⅛″ × 4″ from the black paper for the 3 straight legs. Cut out one leg with a 90° angle. Arrange the tail, legs, and body on the card. When you are satisfied with the placement, paste everything down.

3 Glue the jingle bell into place.

4 Cut out the 2 ears and the head from the black corrugated paper. Glue the head to the body over the gold cord, and glue the ears to the head. Glue the beads on for the eyes.

5 Print the message; frame it and paste it to the card.

Tip

Have a friend who is expecting? Offer to have a party to make birth announcements. Choose one of the projects in this book or design your own. Collect all the supplies. Cut and score the card blanks ahead of time. During the party everyone can chat and paste.

A perfect example of minority rule is a baby in the house.
—Unknown

Supplies

- A 10″ × 7″ card blank in pink and a 9½″ × 6½″ insert, folded.

- A 4¼″ × 6″ piece of green paper background with a deckled edge, pasted to the card front.

- A paper base for the lamb, made using the body template. Use polyester stuffing for the body.

- 4 strips ⅛″ × 4″ from black paper for the legs and a scrap of black paper for the tail.

- A 3″ × 3″ piece of corrugated black paper for the head and ears.

- 2 beads for the eyes.

- A 4″ piece of ⅜″ pink grosgrain ribbon for the bow.

Before starting, read "Techniques," pages 10–17.

Draw the templates freehand or copy the templates on page 77.

How-To

1 Start at the center of the lamb's body base and glue small amounts of stuffing to the base. Work outward until the lamb looks woolly.

2 Cut out the tail and legs. Arrange the tail, legs, and body on the card. When you are satisfied with the placement, paste everything down.

3 Cut out 2 ears and the head from the black corrugated paper. Glue the head to the body and the ears to the head. Glue the beads on for the eyes.

4 Tie a knot in the grosgrain and glue it to the top of the lamb's head. Trim.

5 Print the message and paste it to the card.

Supplies

- A 10″ × 7″ card blank and a 9½″ × 6½″ insert, both folded.

- A 4¼″ × 6¼″ piece of papric or paper for a background, pasted to the card.

- A piece of papric in a mottled chocolate color for the soda.

- A flexible straw.

- Polyester stuffing.

- A small plastic baggie.

- Spray glue.

- A 3¾″ × ⅞″ message frame.

Before starting, read "Techniques," pages 10–17.

Draw the templates freehand or copy the template on page 76.

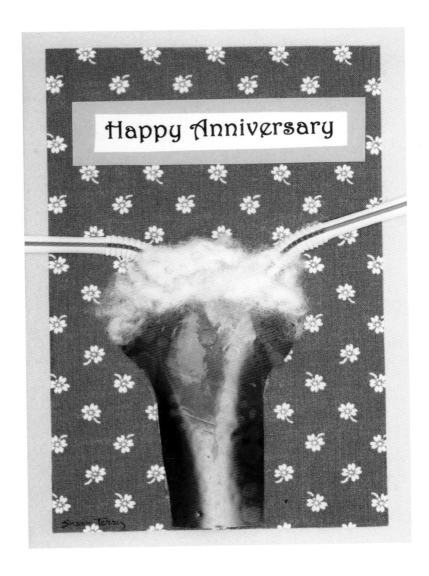

Happy Anniversary

How-To

1 Cut the glass out of the papric. Cut off the seams of the baggie and open it up. Spray the papric glass with the spray glue and press on the baggie. Let dry 5 minutes. Trim the baggie to the papric.

2 Glue a small amount of stuffing to the back center of the glass. Apply glue to the right and left sides of the glass and press to the card. Don't glue the top or bottom. The glass should appear rounded.

3 Use an X-acto knife to slit the straw in half lengthwise. Cut the straw halves down to 3″ in length, with the flexible area in the middle of this.

4 Glue the straws in place. Glue down a small bit of the stuffing to get a "whipped cream" effect.

5 Trim the straws to fit the card.

6 Print the message; frame it and paste it to the card.

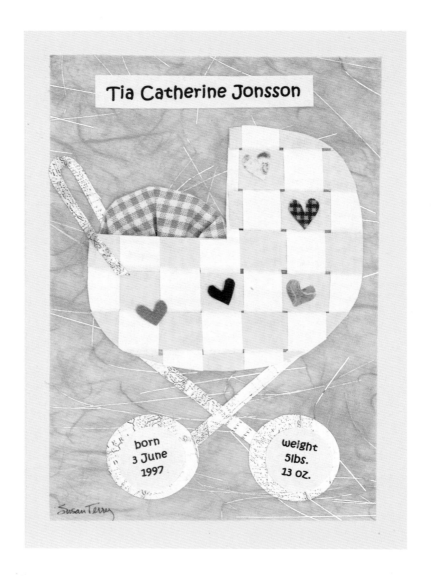

Tia Catherine Jonsson

born
3 June
1997

weight
5lbs.
13 oz.

Tips

For birth announcements, make these cards ahead of time. Once the baby arrives, print the name, weight, and date of birth. Cut out the information out in the shape of wheels and paste these wheels to the card as shown.

Before starting, read "Techniques," pages 10–17.

Draw the templates freehand or copy the card, enlarging it by 125%, and cut the templates out.

If you want a flat-style baby announcement, put the design on a 5″ × 7″ piece of card stock. Use double-sided tape to attach the baby photo to the back of the card.

You can also use two-color "woven" papric for the buggy.

Supplies

- A 10″ × 7″ card blank and a 9½″ × 6½″ insert, both folded.

- A 4¼″ × 6¼″ green paper background, pasted to the card front.

- A 4″ × 4″ square each of white and yellow corrugated paper and a 4″ × 4″ square of white text paper for the buggy base.

- A 4″ × 4″ square of metallic gold paper for the handle, wheels, and support rods.

- A green-and-white plaid fabric cut into a 3″-diameter circle for the blanket.

- 5 little hearts cut freehand.

How-To

1 Cut the yellow corrugated paper into ½″ strips across the corrugation. Cut the white corrugated paper into ½″ strips along the corrugation.

2 Line up the white strips vertically across the paper base. Place these next to each other but don't overlap them. Glue the very top of each strip to the base to hold it in place.

3 Carefully weave the yellow strips into the white strips, pushing them as close to each other as possible. Once a strip is in place, glue down the right and left edges. When finished, glue the bottom of each strip in place.

4 Cut the buggy out of the woven piece. Reglue the edges of the weave to prevent it from coming apart. Paste the hearts to the buggy.

5 Cut out the buggy handle, wheels, and 2 strips ³⁄₁₆″ × 3″ from the metallic gold.

6 Fold the green-and-white plaid fabric circle in half and use a ¼″ seam to shirr the rounded raw edge.

7 Lay the buggy and wheels on the card. Put one end of the handle behind the buggy and the other in front. Cross the strips and put them under the buggy and under the wheels. When you are satisfied with the placement, paste everything down.

8 Use tweezers to pull up the top of the buggy and insert the blanket. You may have to work with the blanket to get it to fit. When it looks right, repaste the buggy back over the blanket.

9 Glue the back of the blanket down.

Babies are such a nice way to start people.
—Don Herold

Supplies

- A 10″ × 7″ card blank and a 9½″ × 6½″ insert, both folded.

- A 4″ × 6″ sky-blue background (papric or paper), pasted to the card.

- A piece of black paper or papric for the mortarboard.

- Red thread and a black circle cut with a hole punch for the tassel.

- 5″ × 5″ green paper for the branches.

- Reverse tweezers.

Before starting, read "Techniques," pages 10–17.

Draw the templates freehand or copy the templates on page 75.

How-To

1 Cut out a combination of 9 branches and paste 6 of them on the left side of the card, varying the lengths. Draw several V-shaped birds, and then paste the remaining 3 branches to the right side of the card, partially covering the birds. Trim the branches along the edges of the card.

2 Cut out the mortarboard and paste it to the card.

3 Cut an index card or a leftover piece of card paper to a 3″ length. Wind the thread around this card a number of times. Slip the thread off the card, hold it together with reverse tweezers, and wrap a length of thread around it about ½″ from the top. Glue the end of this thread down to the back of the tassel. Glue the tassel to the top of the mortarboard and glue the black circle to the top of this.

4 Cut through the bottom loops of the tassel and trim.

Supplies

- A 10″ × 7″ card blank and a 9½″ × 6½″ insert, both folded.

- A 4″ × 5½″ piece of deckled paper, pasted to the card front.

- Papric or paper for the balloons.

- 9″ lengths of yarn or string, one for each balloon string.

- 8″ of ⅛″ ribbon, tied into a bow.

- A 1¾″ × 1⅞″ message frame.

- Packing foam.

- Reverse tweezers.

Before starting, read "Techniques," pages 10–17.

Draw the templates freehand or copy the card, enlarging it by 125%, and cut the templates out.

How-To

1 Cut the balloons out. Glue a string to the back of each one. Paste the background balloons in place.

2 Cut a small circle of the packing foam for each of the 3 foreground balloons. Glue the foam to the backs of the balloons. Glue the foam to the card.

3 Gather up the strings and use the reverse tweezers to hold them together. Adjust the strings until they look right—some should be a little looser than others. Glue the strings to the card at the point where they meet.

4 Glue the bow to the gathered strings. Trim the bow and strings if necessary.

5 Print the message; frame it and paste it to the card.

Before starting, read "Techniques," pages 10–17.

Draw the templates freehand or copy the templates on page 77.

Supplies

- A 10″ × 7″ card blank and a 9½″ × 6½″ insert, both folded.

- A 5½″ × 4¼″ background, pasted to the card blank.

- A second deckled background, 3″ × 4″, pasted to the first background.

- Dried shoots for background foliage. Dry your own or buy them at a craft store.

- A piece of patchwork papric (Method 4) for the elephant and a piece of papric for the ear.

- 1 bead for the eye.

- Stamens.

How-To

1 Glue the dried shoots and stamens to the card.

2 Cut out the elephant and the ear and paste them into place.

3 Glue on the elephant's eye.

Supplies

- A 9″ × 6¼″ card blank and an 8½″ × 5¾″ insert, both folded.

- A 5¾″ × 4″ background of paper or papric, pasted to the card.

- A 5″ × 3¼″ piece of white text paper for the envelope.

- Love stamp.

- Small pieces of leftover papric or paper for the hearts.

- Scribbles Iridescent Gold.

Before starting, read "Techniques,"
pages 10–17.

Draw the templates freehand or
copy the card, enlarging it by 120%,
and cut the templates out.

How-To

1 Fold under ¼″ on both sides of the 3¼″ width of the envelope paper. The paper should now measure 2¾″ × 5″.

2 Fold under 2″ of the 5″ width. Fold 1″ over the top of this. The envelope now measures 2″ × 2¾″.

3 Open up the 1″ fold and cut it to form an envelope flap.

4 Write the message on the envelope front. Paste the sides of the envelope together.

5 Cut and paste a tiny heart to the envelope in the return address position and paste on the stamp. Extend the cancelled lines from the stamp to the envelope.

6 Paste the body of the envelope to the card. Paste the tip of the envelope flap, leaving a small amount of slack.

7 Cut 10 hearts in various sizes and paste them to the card.

8 Apply dollops of Scribbles about ⅜″ apart all around the blue background. Let dry 4 hours.

Supplies

- A 10″ × 7″ card blank and a 9½″ × 6½″ insert, both folded.

- A ⅛″ × 4½″ piece of papric for the clothing rod.

- Scribbles Iridescent Gold for the hanger.

- Sequined papric and lamé papric for the skirt and shirt.

- A postage stamp with a work of art on it. Cut the serration from the stamp.

- Novelty yarn or pearls or beads for the necklace.

- A 1″ × 4″ message frame (left) and a 1¼″ × 3⅜″ frame (right).

Before starting, read "Techniques," pages 10–17.

Draw the templates freehand or copy the card, enlarging it by 125%, and cut the templates out.

How-To

1 With a pencil, lightly draw a hanger at the top of the card blank. Go over it with Scribbles paint. Let dry 4 hours.

2 Cut the rod into 3 parts (refer to the card) and paste.

3 Cut the skirt out of the sequined papric and the shirt out of the lamé. Paste the stamp to the shirt and then paste the skirt and shirt to the card.

4 Print the quote in 2 sections; frame it and paste it to the card.

5 Glue the ends of the necklace to the shirt neck.

··· Tip ···

A work of art on a postage stamp is a witty motif for this card.

Supplies

- A 9″ × 6¼″ card blank and an 8½″ × 5¾″ insert, both folded.

- A 4″ × 5½″ background, deckled and pasted to the front of the card.

- A sequined papric for the hat, a feather, a 1⅜″ piece of ⅛″ ribbon for the hatband, and a button.

- Paprics or papers for the shirt and heart face.

- Gold (or pearl) "necklace" and 2 beads for the earrings.

- A small piece of pink paper or a red pen for the mouth.

- A 3″ × ¾″ message frame.

WE'RE THROWING A PARTY!

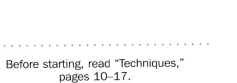

Before starting, read "Techniques," pages 10–17.

Draw the templates freehand or copy the card, enlarging it by 120%, and cut the templates out.

How-To

1 Cut the face, shirt, and hat out of the papric and paste them to the card in that order. Lift up the hat and stick a feather under it. Press down again.

2 Cut a small heart out of the pink paper and paste it in place for the mouth, or draw the mouth with a red pen.

3 Glue down the ends of the hatband. Trim to fit if necessary.

4 Glue the button, earrings, and necklace in place.

5 Print the message; frame it and paste it to the card.

Before starting, read "Techniques," pages 10–17.

Draw the templates freehand or copy the hat template on page 75.

Supplies

- A 10″ × 7″ card blank and a 9½″ × 6½″ insert, both folded.

- A 3¾″ × 6″ background of papric or paper, pasted to the card with the left edge about ½″ inside the edge of the card.

- A 5″ × 3¼″ piece of fabric for the tablecloth, raveled on one of the long ends, and a white doily.

- A ⅛″ × 5½″ piece of black paper for the coat rack post, a ⅛″ × ¾″ piece of black paper for the base, and a scrap of black paper for the 4 hole punches and the cups.

- A small piece of papric or paper for the hat, a small feather, and 3 inches of ⅛″ ribbon for the hatband.

- Papric or paper for the vase.

- Raveled threads and stamens for the flowers.

- A 1⅝″ × 2¼″ message frame.

How-To

1 Paste the coat rack and base to the right of the background paper. Use a black pen to make the 3 U-shaped hooks. Paste 1 hole punch to the top of the rack and the other 3 to the ends of the hooks.

2 Cut out a hat and paste it to the top left hook of the coat rack. Lift up an edge of the hat and stick a feather under it. From the ribbon, cut a hatband to fit the hat and glue both ends. Make a knot in the remainder of the ribbon and glue the knot to the hatband. Trim the ribbon.

3 Turn under ¼″ on the 3 raw edges of the tablecloth and iron down. Shirr the top edge of the tablecloth to a width of 2½″. Glue the shirred edge of the tablecloth to the card. Glue the right and left bottom edges of the tablecloth to the card.

4 Cut a piece of doily to fit the tablecloth top and glue it on.

5 Print the message and paste it to the card. Use a black pen to draw in the picture wire.

6 Cut and paste the vase. Fold 3 stamens in half and stick them under the top edge of the vase. Press into place.

7 Make 4 raveled thread flowers. Glue these to the tops of the stamens.

8 Cut and paste the cups. Draw the handles.

If you haven't got anything nice to say about anybody, come sit next to me.

—Alice Roosevelt Longworth

Before starting, read
"Techniques," pages 10–17.

Draw the templates freehand
or copy the card,
enlarging it by 120%,
and cut the templates out.

Supplies

- A 9″ × 6¼″ card blank and an 8½″ × 5¾″ insert, both folded.

- A 3¾″ × 5″ piece of fabric with ¼″ raveled off all edges and a 3″ × 4¼″ paper base for the placemat.

- A 2¼″-diameter circle from paper or papric for the plate.

- A small piece of paper folded for the place card.

- A 1¾″ square of fabric, with raveled edges, for the napkin.

- Scribbles Iridescent Silver for the silverware.

- A tiny flower and some green paper for leaves.

How-To

1 Apply paste to the placemat base and center it on the back of the placemat. Press into the fabric and let dry. When it is dry, paste it to the card, leaving the raveled edges free.

2 On the back of the plate, draw a smaller circle. Use an X-acto knife to make a slit along the drawn line. Cut around the rest of the circle using scissors. Once cut, trim ⅛″ from the smaller circle. Paste the outside circle and the inside circle to the placemat, slightly to the right of the card center.

3 Fold the napkin until it looks about the right size. Glue the flower stem to the inside of it and glue the napkin to the card. Cut several tiny leaves out of green paper and paste them to the flower stem.

4 Print a name on the place card and paste it into place.

5 Paint the silverware on with Scribbles. Let dry 4 hours.

Basket with Flowers

Lamp

Apple

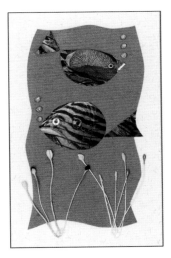

Fish

Hearts

Gift

I save all my leftover small pieces of paper, card paper, papric, and other "unusables" in a box. When I get ready to make gift tags, I get the box and the glue gun out. Tags are fun, and once you start on them, it's hard to stop.

Here's a small gallery of tags to give you some ideas.

Before starting, read "Techniques," pages 10–17.

Draw the templates freehand or copy the cards, enlarging to the desired size, and cut the templates out.

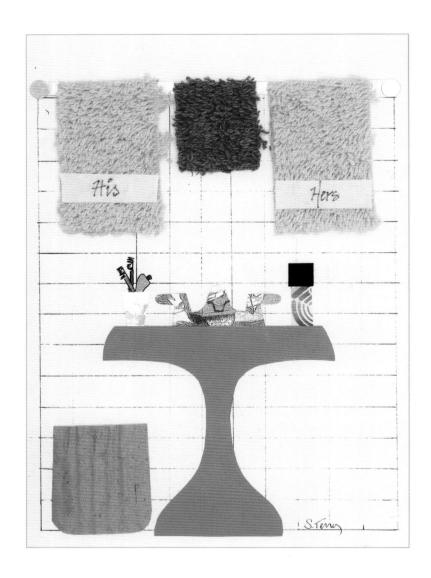

Before starting, read "Techniques," pages 10–17.

Draw the templates freehand or copy the card, enlarging it by 125%, and cut the templates out.

Supplies

- A 10″ × 7″ card blank and a 9½″ × 6½″ insert, both folded.

- Two 1¼″ × 2″ pieces of terrycloth papric in one color and one 1″ × 1¼″ piece of terrycloth papric in another color for the towels and washcloth.

- A 1¼″ × 1½″ piece of corrugated paper for the wastebasket.

- A 4″ × 4″ piece of paper for the sink.

- Two ⅜″ × 1¼″ pieces of white papric or paper for the "His" and "Hers" signs.

- Small pieces of colored paper or stamps for the glass and spray can.

- A 4½″ × 1½″ piece of gold metallic paper for the faucet, towel rack, and finials.

How-To

1 To make a tile background, very lightly draw vertical and horizontal lines on the card, about ½″ apart, using a fine-point black pen. Refer to the card for help with this.

2 Cut out the sink, center it, and paste it ¼″ up from the bottom of the card.

3 Round the 2 bottom corners of the corrugated paper and paste it into place to the left of the sink for the wastebasket.

4 Cut out and paste the faucet to the center of the sink. Cut out a small "glass" and paste it to the left of the faucet.

5 Cut out a very small rectangle for the spray can. Paste it to the right of the faucet. Cut a square slightly larger than the can width for the top. Paste it down.

6 Cut a ³⁄₁₆″ × 4½″ towel rod from the metallic paper. Paste it in place above the sink. The top of the rod should be ¾″ below the top of the card blank. Punch 2 holes from the metallic paper for the "finials" and paste them at the ends of the rod.

7 Paste the towels and washcloth to the rod.

8 Write "His" and "Hers" on the 2 pieces of papric cut for the signs. Paste these toward the bottoms of the towels.

9 Optional: Draw 2 toothbrushes and a tube of toothpaste in the glass.

A wise woman will always let her husband have her way.

—R.B. Sheridan

bon
voyage

Before starting,
read "Techniques,"
pages 10–17.

Draw the templates
freehand or copy the
templates on page 76.

Supplies

- A 10″ × 7″ card blank and a 9½″ × 6½″ insert, both folded.

- Specialty yarn or trim (something with lots of fluff), a 2¾″ circle base cut from paper the same color as the yarn, and a 3″ feather for the bird's body.

- Black paper for the head and legs.

- 2 beads for the eyes.

- A 1⅜″ × 1½″ piece of papric made from a brick fabric for the chimney and a small amount of polyester stuffing for the smoke.

- A 1½″ square message frame and a 3″ piece of thread for the loop.

- A leftover paper towel tube or a small glass.

How-To

1 Wind the yarn around the tube or glass until you think you have enough yarn to make a plump bird. Pull the yarn off the tube, plump it into a circle shape, and glue it to the circle base.

2 Paste on the chimney, slipping a wisp of the stuffing underneath the top of it for "smoke."

3 Cut out the bird's head and 2 legs. On the back of the bird, paste the 2 legs and glue the feather. Glue the body to the card, leaving the legs free.

4 Paste the head into place. Fold the thread in half and stick the fold underneath the bird's beak. Glue on the eyes.

5 Cut two 1½″ × ⅛″ pieces of black paper and paste them to the left side of the card, trimming to fit the card edge.

6 Print the message; frame it and paste it to the card. Stick the thread ends under the frame.

Supplies

- A 10″ × 7″ card blank and a 9½″ × 6½″ insert, both folded.

- A piece of patchwork papric (Method 4) for the sail.

- Blue papric or paper for the waves.

- Papric for the ship.

- A small bit of polyester stuffing for the clouds.

- A 5½″ length of bamboo for the mast.

- A 2¼″ × 1″ message frame for the flag and 2″ of gold ribbon for the flag loop.

- Packing foam.

Before starting, read "Techniques," pages 10–17.

Draw the templates freehand or copy the card, enlarging it by 125%, and cut the templates out.

How-To

1 Paste the stuffing to the top of the card. It should be just thin enough to look like fluffy clouds.

2 Cut out the waves and paste them to the bottom of the card.

3 Cut out the ship and sail. Use the templates to cut a piece of packing foam for each, cutting the foam slightly smaller than the template. Glue the packing foam to the boat and sail.

4 Glue the mast to the foam back of the boat and sail, leaving 2⅝″ of the mast above the sail. Glue the foam to the card.

5 Print a short message and paste it to the flag. Cut out the flag shape. Cut a small piece of packing foam for the back of the flag.

6 Glue the 2 ends of the gold cord to the right edge of the flag to form a loop. Glue the foam to the back of the flag. Slip the loop over the mast and glue the foam to the card.

Before starting, read "Techniques," pages 10–17.

Draw the templates freehand or copy the card, enlarging it by 125%, and cut the templates out.

Time is but the stream I go a-fishing in.
—Thoreau

How-To

1 Print the quote in 2 sections; frame it and paste it to the card.

2 Use a black pen to draw a line from the top of the card to 2″ short of the bottom. Add a U shape for a hook.

3 Cut out the fish and fins and paste them to the card.

4 Use the black pen to make tiny circles above the fishes' mouths. Note that 3 of the fish seem to be asking a question.

5 Cut reed shapes out of papric and paste them along the bottom. Glue on several pieces of raffia and a few stamens. Use the pen to lightly draw in some grasses between the "reeds."

6 Optional: Draw a little worm on the fishhook.

Supplies

- A 6½″ × 5″ card blank and a 6″ × 4½″ insert, both folded.

- Small buttons, fringe, raveled threads, snaps, beads, and green yarn.

- Leftover green and brown papric or paper.

- A large button or sequin "spokes."

Before starting, read "Techniques," pages 10–17.

Draw the templates freehand or copy the card and cut the templates out.

S.Terry

How-To

1 Glue down green yarn or paper for stems.

2 Glue buttons, snaps, and/or tiny bells down to make "flowers."

3 Cut several styles of leaves from the green paprics. Glue them around the stems and at the base of the card.

4 Make several flower shapes from raveled thread and glue them down. Glue a bead in the center of each. With a pen, draw some stems and leaves.

5 Cut a small piece of fringe and glue it into a circle. Glue a spoke or button into the center of this circle.

6 Cut 2 narrow strips of brown and glue them to the bottom of the card.

···· Tip ····

*This is a small card made using a glue gun and left-overs. You probably don't have the same leftovers that I have, but everyone has **something** left over. Use your imagination to create a similar card.*

Youth is like spring,

an overpraised season.

Samuel Butler.

Supplies

- A 10″ × 7″ card blank and a 9½″ × 6½″ insert, both folded.

- A 4″ × 6″ "rainy" background, pasted to the card front.

- Papric in 2 different golds for the daisies and raveled threads.

- Green paprics and green raffia for the leaves and stems.

- Beads and stamens for the flower centers.

- A 2½″ × ¾″ message frame (top), a 2¾″ × ¾″ frame (bottom), and a 1¼″ × ⅜″ frame (for the quote author's name).

Before starting, read "Techniques," pages 10–17.

Draw the templates freehand or copy the card, enlarging it by 125%, and cut the templates out.

How-To

1 Cut and paste the 2 daisy stems to the card. Knot an 8″ piece of raffia every inch. Glue the bottom and top of this to the card for the raveled thread flower stem.

2 Cut out and paste the leaves to the card.

3 Cut out and paste the daisy petals to the card. Cut small triangles and paste them to the base of the daisies. Insert several stamens underneath the drooping daisy petals.

4 Make 2 raveled thread flowers. Glue them to the card so that they look as if they are being blown about in the wind. Glue beads to the centers of these.

5 Print the quote in 3 sections as shown; frame it and paste it to the card.

Tip

If you don't have a fabric with a rainy theme, use gray paper. Paint Scribbles Iridescent Silver in slanted, interrupted lines across it. Let the paper dry 4 hours and use it as the background for this card.

Supplies

- A 10″ × 7″ card blank and a 9½″ × 6½″ insert, both folded.

- A 5″ × 5″ piece of green papric for the background grass and tree branches.

- A 4½″ square of corrugated white paper for the fence.

- Small bits of paper for the birdhouse, roof, and chimney.

- A ⅛″ × 3½″ piece of paper for the birdhouse pole.

- Stamens and raffia for the grass.

- A ¾″ × 2″ message frame and a 4″ piece of gold thread for the hanger.

Before starting, read "Techniques," pages 10–17.

Draw the templates freehand or copy the card, enlarging it by 125%, and cut the templates out.

Templates for the branches are on page 75.

How-To

1 Cut a 4¾″ × 1¼″ piece of the green papric and paste it near the bottom of the card blank.

2 Paste the birdhouse pole to the card. Cut out the birdhouse, punch a hole in it, and paste it into place with a tiny bit of fabric behind the hole. Cut the roof and chimney and paste them into place.

3 Cut the white paper into six ¼″ × 2⅝″ posts and two ¼″ × 4½″ crossbars. Glue down the ends of the crossbars. Glue the tops and bottoms of the posts in place.

4 Split the raffia into narrow lengths. Glue these and the stamens around the fence posts and birdhouse pole.

5 Make the branches out of the green papric. Paste them to the card, looping the gold thread over the end of one of the branches. Trim the left edge of the card.

6 Print the message; frame it and paste it to the card. Place the looped gold threads under the frame.

Before starting, read "Techniques," pages 10–17. Draw the templates freehand or copy the template on page 75.

Supplies

- A 10″ × 7″ card blank and a 9½″ × 6½″ insert, both folded.

- A 4″ × 6″ piece of deckled paper for a background, pasted to the card.

- A piece of patchwork papric (Method 4) for the pumpkin, made with browns, golds, reds, oranges, and greens.

- Green paprics or papers for the leaves.

- Gold tinsel on a spool for the vines. You could also use a lightweight gold cord or ribbon, or draw the vines in.

- A 1″ twig from your yard.

- Reverse tweezers.

How-To

1 Cut the pumpkin out of the patchwork papric and cut it along the lines indicated on the pattern.

2 Paste the pumpkin pieces to the card. From the left, the first and second pieces should touch at the bottom and be open at the top. The second and third pieces should touch at the top and be open at the bottom. Continue on in this way until the pumpkin pieces are pasted on.

3 Cut out 5 pumpkin leaves and paste them on. Glue the twig in place at the top of the pumpkin.

4 Hold the end of the tinsel with reverse tweezers. Twist the tweezers 5–7 times to wind the tinsel around the tweezers. Cut and remove the tinsel from the tweezers. Glue the ends to the card to make "vines." Repeat 4 times.

The older the tree,
the sweeter the sap.

Vermont proverb

Before starting, read "Techniques," pages 10–17.

Draw the templates freehand or copy the card, enlarging it by 125%, and cut the templates out.

Supplies

- A 10″ × 7″ card blank and a 9½″ × 6½″ insert, both folded.
- A 4⅝″ × 5¾″ black background pasted to the card front, and a 4¼″ × 5¼″ light background pasted to the black background.
- Papric or paper in a mottled brown for the tree.
- Green papric and paper for the leaves and stems.
- Raveled threads for the flowers.
- A 2″ × 1″ message frame.

How-To

1 Cut out the tree and paste it to the card.

2 Cut the small tree leaves freehand out of the greens and paste them to the tree branches.

3 Cut a few long reeds out of papric or paper and paste them around the trunk of the tree.

4 Make 2 raveled thread flowers.

5 Print the quote; frame it and paste it to the card.

Before starting, read "Techniques," pages 10–17.

Draw the templates freehand or copy the card, enlarging it by 115%, and cut the templates out.

Supplies

For either card:

- An 8½″ × 5½″ card blank and an 8″ × 5″ insert, both folded.

- A 3⅝″ × 4⅞″ background piece, pasted to the card blank.

- A 3¼″ × 4¼″ piece of corrugated paper, glued to the background.

- A variety of red and green paprics for the fruit and leaves.

- A piece of corrugated white or cream paper for the core and a ¼″ × 3″ strip of black paper for the seeds.

- A small twig from your yard.

How-To

1 Cut out the fruit and leaves. Use an X-acto knife to cut out the core.

2 Cut a piece of corrugated paper (the corrugation should be horizontal) a bit larger than the removed core. On the back of the apple or pear, glue the corrugated paper, covering the hole.

3 Paste the apple or pear to the background.

4 Glue the twig to the top of the fruit and paste on the leaves.

5 Cut the seeds from the black paper. These are small, and tweezers will really help. Glue the seeds to the core.

Few things are harder to put up with than the annoyance of a good example.

—Mark Twain

Supplies

- A 10″ × 7″ card blank and a 9½″ × 6½″ insert, both folded.

- A 4½″ × 6″ piece of papric in a Halloween-themed fabric for a background, pasted to the card front.

- A piece of black papric for the cat.

- A small piece of gold papric or paper for the moon.

- A piece of brown papric for the mountain.

- A 5½″ bamboo stick (or a small, straight twig) for the broom handle.

- 3″ cuts of raffia (20–30) for the broom.

- 2 small beads for the eyes.

- Five 4″ lengths of black thread for the whiskers.

- Reverse tweezers.

- White pencil to mark the cat's nose.

How-To

1 Cut out the mountain and moon. Paste in place.

2 Hold the cut pieces of raffia together with reverse tweezers. Wrap a piece of raffia around this bundle, about 1″ from the top. Slip the bamboo stick in and knot the raffia.

3 Cut out the cat. Position the cat and the broom on the card; the cat's tail should be on top of the broom. Paste the cat down, leaving the end of the tail free.

4 Glue the broom into place. Glue the cat's tail over it.

5 Glue the beads on for the eyes.

6 Use the white pencil to draw a triangle-shaped nose on the cat.

7 Hold the lengths of black thread together and tie a knot in the center. Glue the knot to the bottom of the cat's nose. Fluff the threads out to look like whiskers, and trim.

Before starting, read "Techniques," pages 10–17.

Draw the templates freehand
or copy the templates on page 77.

Supplies

- A 10″ × 7″ card blank and a 9½″ × 6½″ insert, both folded.

- Five 5¾″ lengths of bamboo and two 4″ lengths for the trellis (or cut some twigs to this size).

- 5–6 green paprics for leaves and gourd tops.

- Patchwork papric (Method 4) in orange, red, gold, and green for the gourds. If you've made the pumpkin card, you should have enough left over for the gourds on this card.

- Black thread for the vines. Use carpet or quilting thread if you have it.

Before starting, read "Techniques," pages 10–17.

Draw the templates freehand or copy the card, enlarging it by 125%, and cut the templates out.

How-To

1 Arrange the 5 long pieces of bamboo vertically and glue the ends of each to the card. Arrange the shorter bamboo sticks horizontally and glue them to the vertical sticks where they touch.

2 Cut out 10 gourd leaves. Glue them down.

3 Cut 4 gourds out of the patchwork papric. Glue them down.

4 Cut little green triangles out of papric or paper for the tops of the gourds. Glue in place.

5 Wind lengths of black thread around and through the trellis until you like the effect. Glue the thread in various spots to hold it in place.

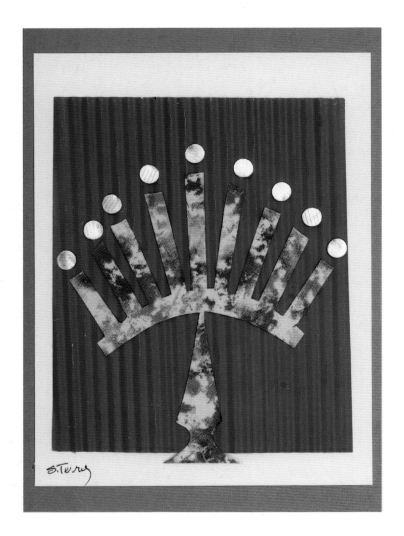

Before starting, read "Techniques," pages 10–17.

Draw the templates freehand or copy the card, enlarging it by 120%, and cut the templates out.

Supplies

- A 9″ × 6¼″ blue card blank and an 8½″ × 5¾″ insert, both folded.

- A 4¼″ × 5½″ white or cream background, pasted to the card blank.

- A 3¾″ × 4½″ piece of corrugated blue paper, glued to the background.

- Blue papric for the menorah.

- 9 punch holes from gold metallic paper for the candle flames.

How-To

1 Cut the menorah out of the blue papric and paste it to the corrugated background.

2 Glue the punch holes to the tops of the candles.

···· **Tip** ····

Make this design into a candelabra by changing the colors or number of candles.

Supplies

- A 9″ × 6¼″ card blank and an 8½″ × 5¾″ insert, both folded.

- A 4¼″ × 5½″ background, pasted to the card blank.

- A piece of "woven" papric (Method 3) in Christmas colors for the ornament.

- A ½″ square of gold paper for the ornament top and a 2½″ piece of gold tie for the hook.

- Two 3½″ pieces of wired greenery for the fir branch.

- Packing foam.

Before starting, read "Techniques," pages 10–17.

Draw the templates freehand or copy the card, enlarging it by 120%, and cut the templates out.

Merry   Christmas

Susan Terry

How-To

1 "Droop" the greenery and glue the ends of it to the top of the card.

2 Loop the gold tie around the greenery and glue the ends to the card.

3 Glue the ornament top over the ends of the gold tie.

4 Cut the ornament out. Cut a piece of packing foam slightly smaller than the ornament and glue it to the ornament back. Glue the foam to the card.

5 Print the message in 2 sections and paste it to the card.

Tip

Draw and cut the ornament in any shape—for example, diamond, triangle, circle, or onion-shaped (as shown).

Supplies

- A 10″ × 7″ card blank and a 9½″ × 6½″ insert, both folded.

- A 4½″ × 6¼″ background, pasted to the card front.

- A 3¾″ × 5½″ piece of handmade paper, deckled and pasted to the background.

- 2 shades of green paper and a 5/16″ × 1″ piece of brown paper for the tree and trunk.

- 3″ of gold thread for tree decorations.

- Red, gold, and green paper for punch holes and other shapes.

- Paper or papric for gifts and red and green raffia for bows.

- Papric and gold metallic paper for hearts and stars.

How-To

1 Paste the trunk to the card. Cut out 2 larger triangles from the lighter green and 1 smaller triangle from the dark green. Paste them to the card.

2 Cut out and paste the gifts. Make tiny bows and glue them to the tops of the gifts.

3 Cut out and punch out the tree "decorations." Paste some a bit under the branches and some on the tree. Glue the ends of the gold thread to the tree and glue a number of punched holes to the thread. Cut out and paste on the hearts and star.

4 With a pen, draw tiny hooks on the ornaments.

5 Print a message and paste it to a gift.

· ·

Before starting, read "Techniques," pages 10–17.

Draw the templates freehand or copy the card, enlarging it by 125%, and cut the templates out.

· ·

Supplies

- A 10″ × 7″ card blank and a 9½″ × 6½″ insert, both folded.

- A 4¼″ × 6″ deckled background, pasted to the card front.

- Corrugated white paper for the snowman.

- Paper or papric for the hat and scarf.

- A 4¼″ piece of bamboo and a blade of saw grass cut into 2″ pieces (or raffia) for the broom.

- Twigs from your yard for the arms.

- Orange and black paper for the nose, eyes, and buttons.

- Wired greenery for the bush.

- Gold metallic paper and a 2″ length of gold thread for the bush decoration.

- Aleene's Glitter Snow and a toothpick.

- A ⅞″ × 1″ message frame.

Before starting, read "Techniques," pages 10–17.

Draw the templates freehand or copy the templates on page 75.

How-To

1 Cut out the snowman and hat and paste them to the card.

2 Glue the broom handle and saw grass to the card.

3 Glue the twigs. The snowman's right arm goes over the broom.

4 Cut out the eyes, buttons, and nose and glue them on.

5 Cut and paste the scarf and knot.

6 Cut several small pieces of greenery and glue them to look like a bush.

7 Punch several small holes from the gold paper. Glue 1 hole to each end of the gold thread and then glue the holes to the bush. Cut out several small round, square, or diamond shapes and glue them to the thread to look like ornaments.

8 Print the message in 2 sections; frame it and paste it to the card.

9 Use a toothpick and your finger to apply snow around the base of the snowman, broom, and bush.

Candles

Gift

Topiary

Christmas Tree

Bell

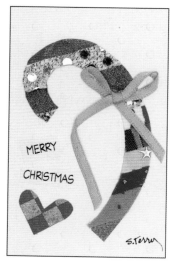

Candy Cane

Every year I have great fun with these Christmas tags; they're simple to make and dress up even the most plainly wrapped Christmas present. Besides putting them on packages, I use them for place cards at Christmas dinner. During the holiday season, when I need a small gift, I tie a ribbon around 5 of these for a hostess or a friend.

Cut a few squares and rectangles for gifts and candles, cut triangles for trees, cut any odd shape you want for bells, and put all of it together with the glue gun. Here's a gallery of tags to give you ideas.

Before starting, read "Techniques," pages 10–17.

Draw the templates freehand or copy the card, enlarging to your desired size, and cut the templates out.

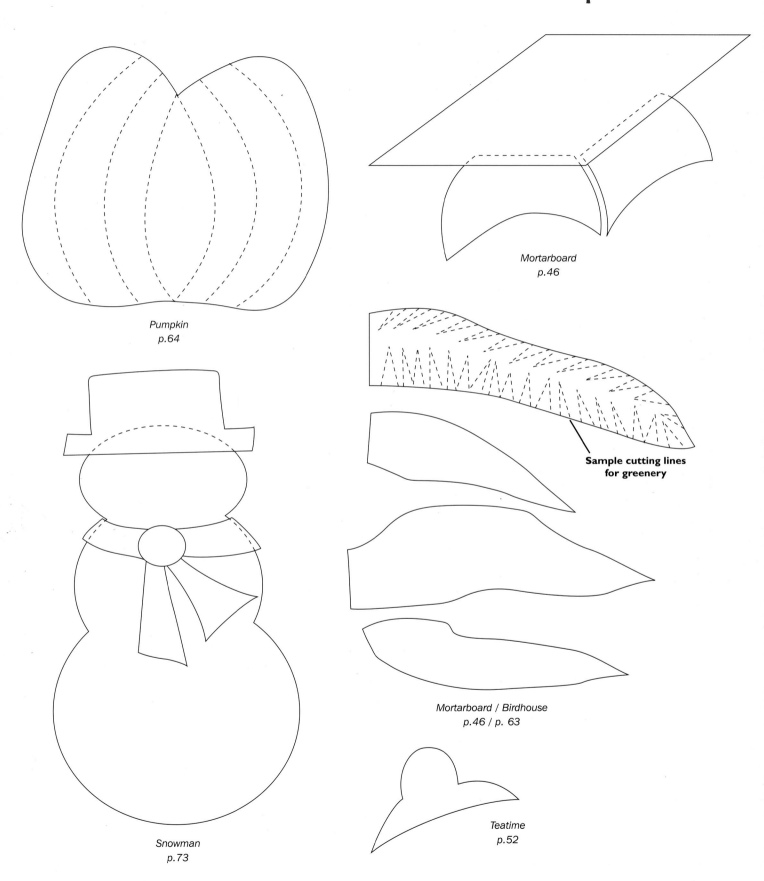

Pumpkin
p.64

Mortarboard
p.46

**Sample cutting lines
for greenery**

Mortarboard / Birdhouse
p.46 / p. 63

Snowman
p.73

Teatime
p.52

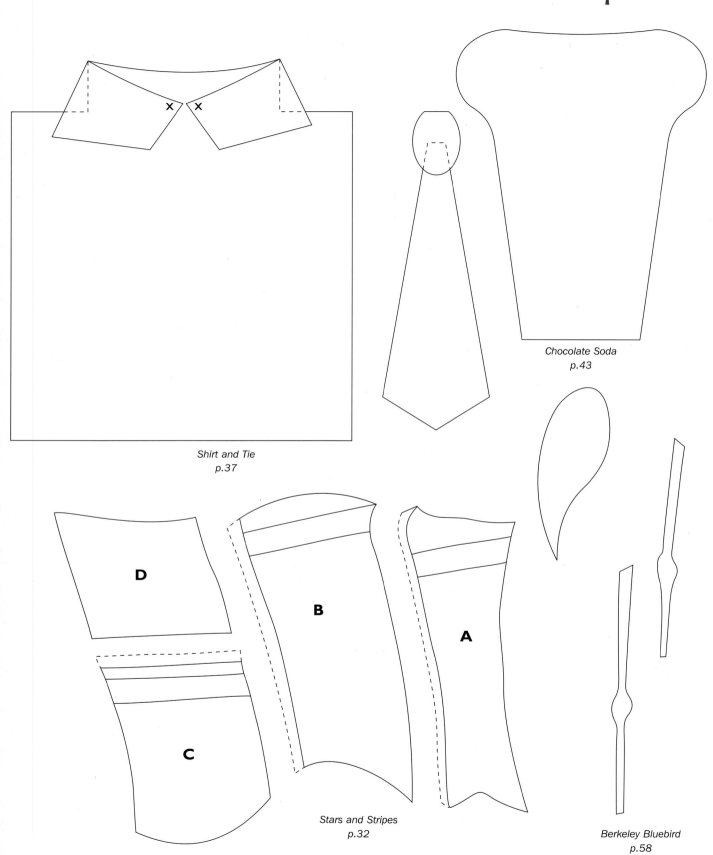

Shirt and Tie
p.37

Chocolate Soda
p.43

D

B

C

A

Stars and Stripes
p.32

Berkeley Bluebird
p.58

Little Elephant
p.48

Cradle Card
p.23

**Lamb's
ear**

**Lamb's
head**

**Lamb's
body**

It's a Boy! / It's a Girl!
pp.40–42

Black Cat
p.68

index

acknowledgments

My greatest thanks to my husband, Brent, who gives me the support and time I need to work on the things I love.

And special thanks to Lee Jonsson, my editor, who patiently helped me work out the details of this book. When my confidence in my design abilities flagged, she propped me up and egged me on.

And to the staff at C&T Publishing, thank you for the contribution of all your skills. The book would not exist without your impressive efforts.

about the author

Susan S. Terry describes herself as a determined optimist. She began her cardmaking career by promising her mother 75 handmade invitations for a 50th anniversary celebration. "How hard could it be? No problem."

By the time she managed to actually produce the invitations, Susan was hooked on cardmaking. A quilter in possession of unlimited fabric scraps, she eventually developed a simple process for turning these scraps into paper to use in handmade cards. Whether it's fabric or paper; beads, buttons, or bows; leftover or new, Susan makes a card from it.

Susan lives with her cards and her husband, Brent, in Oakland, California.

resources

Stamens can be purchased from:
Jennifer Osner
www.jenniferosner.com
(415) 239-5896

other books by Susan S. Terry

Great Titles
from
C&T PUBLISHING